About this Guide

Minecraft is a sandbox game originally developed by Swedish video game programmer Markus 'Notch' Persson. The game was inspired by other, older, classic games like Dwarf Fortress, Dungeon Keeper and Infinminer. At its most basic, Minecraft is a block based construction game. However the beauty of Minecraft is in the sandbox Survival elements. The player is not limited to just building. Elements of survival game play like collecting resources and food, crafting weapons, armor and potions and fighting hostile mobs as well as other players, make the simplistic game much much more than the sum of its parts.

The Survival mode is dedicated to this kind of game play. On Survival Multiplayer servers you can actually play with other players, be it in co-ordination with them, or against them. Player vs player servers are very popular too. Some have a certain set of rules that control the chaos, other servers are rougher, with no holds barred combat that can get very intense and dirty at times.

One thing that is common in such servers is enemy players raiding each other's' bases in order to loot resources or to simply grief the opposing party. Since other player can wait and raid your base at times when you are not online, it is not always possible to personally prevent such occurrences. In such times traps are your best friends.

Traps can not only help you add extra lines of defense to your base, but they can also give you an edge in combat if your base is attacked while you are inside. If designed properly most traps can be made more or less invisible, making them extremely dangerous to new and headstrong players.

This guide contains all the basic types of traps that can be created in Minecraft. Most of these traps can be modified to make them bigger and more effective and more suited to your own needs.

To create some of these traps you will need some working knowledge of Redstone circuits. A few tips and tricks pertaining to the subject are given along with the trap tutorials. In the end no matter what kind of traps you choose to construct make sure you do not forget to use a little bit of your own imagination, to get even better results.

I hope you enjoy reading and using this guide as much as I enjoyed writing it.

Basics of Trapping

Traps in Minecraft are comprised of three parts. The *trigger*, which is used to activate the trap. A *mechanism*, which is connected to the trigger and relays the input from the trigger to the last part of the trap, which is the *method*. The method is the part that actually traps or kills the entity (player or mob) that has activated the trap.

Trigger

Triggers can comprise of any of the following -

1. Pressure plates
2. Levers
3. Buttons
4. Tripwires
5. Daylight sensors

A combination of these triggers can also be used. An item can be placed on a pressure plate to push it down. When a player walks into the room and picks up the item, the pressure plate deactivates, breaking the signal. This can be used with an inverter to create any kind of trap.

A point to note when using triggers is that they need to be hidden in plain sight. They should be at a place where the entity can access them. This is particularly important when creating traps for other players.

One way to get players to activate the trigger is to use some lure. Lures in Minecraft are limited to some rare items like diamonds, gold ingots or enchanted weapons/ books. However such greed based lures do not work on advanced and cautious players. More often than not, carefully placed traps use the player's innate curiosity as a lure.

Mechanism

The next part of the trap, the mechanism, usually comprises of Redstone circuits.

1. Redstone circuits like a clock circuit can be used to produce a periodic pulse. Useful mechanism for automated mob traps.

2. Inverter circuits using Redstone torches are used with reverse triggers like the weighted pressure plate with the item on it.

3. Water flow can be used as a mechanism, especially against mobs.

4. Falling sand or gravel can also be used as a mechanism.

While the trigger should be accessible, mechanisms need to be hidden and inaccessible to the entity. A trap where the mechanism is visible in the final stage is poorly designed and has a high chance of getting disarmed before it can kill/ trap its target.

Method

The final part of the trap is the method which is used to kill/ trap the entity. The list of methods is large and you can be quite creative with it.

1. Falling into pits. Simple and effective, especially against mobs, this method uses fall damage to kill its target. Slightly harder to use versus other players when pits are visible. Can be countered using false floors.

2. Water. It can be used to drown entities. In case of using water care must be taken that the area where the entity is to be drowned must be enclosed so that water does not seep out and damage the trap itself.

3. Lava. Dangerous and effective. Lava based killing traps are more or less similar in design to water based traps. Again care must be taken that lava does not seep out of the killing area. Also care must be taken while working with lava lest you end up dying yourself.

4. Suffocation. Dropping two blocks of sand or gravel on top of players will bury them and cause them to take damage. Same thing happens if any opaque block is forced on the top half of any entity. For instance trapping an entity in a two block high space and then using a piston to push a cobblestone block in the upper block where the player is, will cause damage.

5. Arrows. Firing them from dispensers can create simple and effective arrow traps. They make for quick kills and are hard to avoid once triggered.

6. Cactus causes damage to all entities that come too close. Forcing mobs into a grid of cacti is another method that can be use to kill them.

Again this is not effective against other players because they can break the cacti and escape.

7. Mobs. Trapping players in a large dark room where hostile mobs can spawn is another way to kill them. While this method is slightly unreliable, it can allow you to combine a mob farm with a trap.

8. Dynamite. Last but not the least is TNT. Makes for very fun and explosive traps, and once a bunch of TNT blocks are triggered it is near enough impossible to escape the area unscathed. The downside is that the result explosion is likely to destroy a lot of the surrounding area, including the trap itself. This means that TNT traps are more of a one time use thing and need to be rebuilt every time.

TNT Based Traps

In this section we will build the traps that use TNT as the *method*. These traps usually need to be re made after every use, or are more of a last resort thing, like the DEFCON trap which can be used to destroy your whole base with the enemies inside it.

TNT Mine

What you will need -

1. TNT blocks
2. Pressure plates
3. Any kind of solid block (preferably one which matches the ground/ floor)
4. Sand/ Gravel blocks

The simplest TNT based trap there is. All you need to do is a dig a hole two blocks deep. At the bottom place a block of TNT. On top of it place a covering block. On top of that place a pressure plate.

The moment the pressure plate is activated the TNT below it too will get activated and explode after a few seconds, blowing up the player who stepped on it, and a huge chunk of your floor along with them.

The down side of this trap is that any player who is paying even half the attention to the game is bound to hear the hissing of the dynamite once it activates, and they will have a few moments to run to safety.

This can be countered by making the mine large. That is place multiple blocks of dynamite in a small cluster below one pressure plate. This will make the explosion area larger, making the chance of the player getting damaged higher. Another way is to make the TNT mine more advanced by changing its design a little.

What we do is we dig the hole, at least three blocks deep. On the middle block we place the TNT block leaving one block of empty space below it. On top of TNT we place a block like Sand or Gravel. On top of that place the pressure plate.

Now when the player activates the pressure plate, it will activate the TNT. Activated TNT falls like Sand and gravel unless supported. Thus since the block below it is empty, it will fall. The Sand/ gravel block above it will lose its support and it too will fall. As will the entity standing on the Sand/ Gravel block.

So basically the moment the pressure plate is activated whoever is standing on it, will fall into the hole with an active TNT block below them. Now, while it might be still possible for someone with presence of mind to quickly place a block below them, jump out and run, it is far less likely that they will be successful in escaping the blast. To this end, the deeper you dig the hole, the better. The TNT will always be second block from the top.

The drawback of this design is that the top block needs to be Sand or Gravel. Thus it is more likely to be noticed, unless the entire floor is made out of such blocks. One way to hide it in plain sight is to make the floor out of Sandstone or Cobblestone, and use Sand and Gravel blocks respectively.

Pressure Plate Maze Trap

What you will need -

1. Pressure plates
2. TNT blocks
3. Solid blocks matching the floor

This is a modified and more sophisticated trap based on the TNT mine design. In fact this is more of a hindrance than a real trap.

I am sure many of you must remember the *Name of God* stepping stones trap from Indiana Jones and the Last Crusade. This is kind of similar to that. What we need is a large room, as shown below. At least seven blocks long and five blocks wide.

Now leaving one block space between the doorways leading into the room on both sides, dig a hole, five by five blocks, and at least two blocks deep.

Place TNT blocks in any pattern which suits your fancy. Make sure the empty spaces you leave between TNT blocks are connected. Form a path using the empty spaces from one side of the room to the other. A simple example is given in the screencap below. The larger the room, the more complex a path you can create. But make sure the path is not too complex for you to remember yourself.

Next cover the entire TNT layer with a layer of solid blocks. On top place a grid of pressure plates.

Your trap is ready. Now the only way to cross the room is to know the safe path through the pressure plates. As long as you step on the plates with not TNT below them, everything will be fine. The moment someone steps on a plate with a TNT block below it, the TNT gets activated, and boom. The entire room is blown into smithereens.

Excellent trap to place in an adventure based dungeon or your medieval castle's entrance.

Double Lever Rail Trap

What you need -

1. TNT mine cart

2. Redstone dust

3. Two levers

4. One block Activator rail

5. Powered rails

6. A Sticky piston

7. A mine cart/ rail network for entry into your base

This trap is perfect if your base access is via an underground mine cart and rail network, or even if you simply want to make sure that only those with authorization can use a particular rail network.

What you need to do is, add a parallel rail line to the original rail line. The second rail line will be hidden and will always have a TNT mine cart at its starting.

The trick will be that we are going to connect the activation trigger for the original rail with the line on which the TNT mine cart is. This second rail line is going to intersect the original rail line at some point at least a dozen blocks away from the starting terminal.

Now whenever someone activates the rail to travel they will inadvertently activate the TNT mine cart too, which will start moving and eventually reach the intersection point with the original line. Just before the intersection point will be an activator rail, which will activate the TNT. When the TNT mine cart blows up, it will kill whoever is traveling on the original line.

To make sure that authorized players can travel safely, we will add a simple circuit breaker made out of a sticky piston, and controlled by a second hidden lever. Whenever you want to use the rail, you activate the piston, breaking the connection between the activation trigger of the original line and the TNT mine cart, making the line safe for use.

To begin with place the blocks as shown below. To the right is the original rail line. To the left is the hidden line on which the TNT mine cart is going to be. In the center is the sticky piston based circuit breaker.

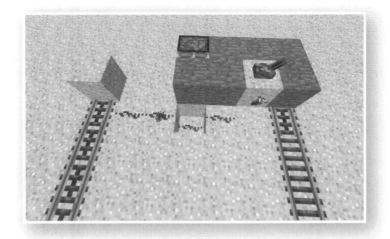

Make sure you hide the secondary line from sight. Also try to hide the piston and the lever that will activate the breaker in a room away from the boarding terminal for the original line. This way only players who know where it is can use it.

When the breaker is activated, the connection will break, making the line safe to travel.

If it is not activated, the lever used to activate the original line will activate the secondary line too.

Make the intersection something like what is shown below. Note the activator rail.

When a player tries to use the original line without activating the circuit breaker, the TNT filled mine cart will intercept them and blow up in their face.

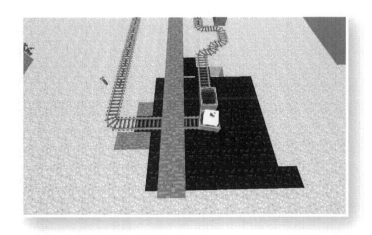

The critical thing in this trap is first to make sure that the circuit breaker switch is hidden well out of sight so that it is not accidentally discovered. Secondly and just as importantly, is setting the timing, so that the TNT mine cart reaches the intersection and explodes just as the mine cart bearing the player does. There are a variety of ways to tweak the speeds of the mine carts. You can add some additional loops to increase timing, or simply lower the speed by using fewer powered rails. You can use inclines to increase speed or just design the lines in a way that the player bearing mine cart has to travel longer.

All in all, if made properly this trap has very few disadvantages. Only the most cautious players will suspect foul play if everything is hidden properly. Furthermore, once the players are in a mine cart traveling at high speed, even if they do realize something is wrong, chances are they will not be able to react in time to escape.

The only drawback is that when the TNT mine cart explodes, it will take a chunk of the network with it, so you will have to replace a few blocks of tracks every time. This damage can be minimized by using Obsidian blocks at the intersection of the two lines.

Explosive Pond of Death

What you will need -

1. TNT blocks

2. Water buckets

3. Some solid blocks

4. Pressure plates

This is a funny little trap which has limited use but great potential for surprise. It is useful against players who like to fish.

First dig a simple nine by nine block hole, at least five blocks deep.

At the bottom place a layer of TNT blocks.

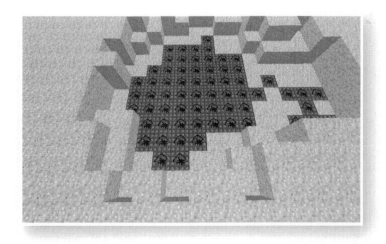

Cover the layer of TNT blocks with a layer of solid blocks. Something like Sand or Gravel is good.

Cover the whole base with pressure plates.

Fill the hole with water. Remember that water blocks can only be placed a block above the pressure plates. The block containing the plate will remain empty.

Now when a player tries to fish in the pond, the pressure plates will get activated and in turn activate the TNT. The TNT will blow up causing damage.

The potential for damage in this trap is slightly low because explosions in water do not break blocks and cause reduced damage. However, using light blocks like sand or gravel on the banks will slightly increase the damage potential.

DEFCON Fail-safe trap

What you will need -

1. A lot of TNT
2. A trigger

This is a last resort measure meant for times when no other alternative is left. The enemies are in your base and looting everything you have collected. You cannot stop them no matter what you do. You are out numbered. You would rather see everything destroyed once and for all, than let it fall into the hands of your enemies. That is the kind of situation this trap is meant for.

Basically you rig your entire base with TNT. Preferably below the floor of your base. And you connect it with one very very well hidden trigger, like a lever, or a button.

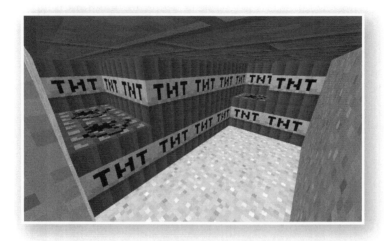

When all is lost and you see no other alternative, reach the trigger and activate it. All of your base will blow up and be destroyed, and with it, your enemies who were inside too will be destroyed.

Simply place a layer of TNT below your base.

Connect it to the trigger using redstone dust. If you want to survive the explosion yourself make sure you hide the trigger room a little way away from your base, or make it out of Obsidian.

When the time comes, flip the lever and get ready to start over from nothing.

Greedy miner TNT trap

What you will need -

1. A couple of Daylight sensors.
2. TNT blocks.
3. Some diamond ore blocks/ any kind of rare and precious blocks.
4. Redstone dust

This trap uses precious blocks to lure players. Blocks are placed out in the open. Below the blocks is a daylight sensor rigged to a lot of TNT. The moment the block is broken and light reaches the daylight sensor, it will activate the TNT causing it to explode. Because of its design this trap is risky to make during day time, as once the daylight sensor is placed you might accidentally blow yourself up before covering it. It is thus better to make this trap during night time.

The trap can be designed in a variety of ways. The most effective is placing the lure blocks as the floor in an open area without a roof (or a clear glass roof), as shown below.

First dig a hole. Make it as large as you want, but keep it only two blocks deep.

Place TNT blocks at the bottom. Leave out a space in one corner for the sensor.

Place the sensor and connect it to TNT using redstone wiring.

Cover the whole thing with solid opaque blocks. Right on top of the sensor place the block that will act as the lure.

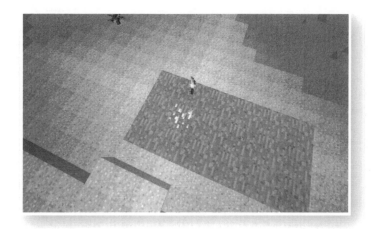

After this trap is rigged, never make the mistake of opening it during day time as the TNT will get activated the moment light reaches the daylight sensor. If you absolutely must do it, then try going in from the side and breaking the TNT blocks first.

The only disadvantage of this trap is that it does not work if the lure block is broken during night time.

Water and Lava Based Traps

This section is a compilation of all traps that use water or lava to drown and kill their victims. Since both fluids break items on contact, (specially lava which burns everything in its way) it is important that containment area is built around these traps.

Lava room of death trap

What you will need -

1. Four buckets of lava
2. Four sticky pistons
3. Redstone torch
4. Restone dust
5. A lever
6. Doors

This trap tricks the player into thinking that the lever is the trigger to open a door, while it is actually a trigger to open the fake ceiling, made using sticky pistons. Above the fake ceiling is a reservoir of lava, which will flow down and fill the room, setting the player on fire and in all probability, killing them.

To make this trap build a simple room with two by two block space. Place doors at both ends. Also place a lever a block away from the exit door.

Place sticky pistons on the ceiling level as shown below.

On the other side of the wall, corresponding to the lever, place a redstone torch. This will create a simple inverter that will keep the pistons activated when the lever as deactivated. As soon as the lever is flipped, the pistons will deactivate and retract, opening the ceiling.

Connect the four pistons as shown below.

Fill the reservoir with four buckets of lava.

Now as soon as any one flips the lever, the ceiling will open and the room will be flooded with lethal stream of lava. Once the lever burns away, the ceiling will close once more, and the lever will need to be replaced, but the damage will already be done.

Water Whirlpool Trap

What you will need -

1. Four to nine blocks of TNT
2. Stack of sand or gravel

Unlike many other traps in the guide, this one is mainly for mobs, and it is more of a barrier than a trap.

If your base includes entrance via a water body, and you want to prevent random mobs swimming into your base through it, then this trap is extremely helpful.

Thing is it is hard to build gates in water, so instead we build a whirlpool. While other players can traverse it using a boat, or even swim across it with a little care, most mobs will simply sink to the bottom.

The way to make this trap is to first create a hollow column of sand, four by four blocks, right to the bottom of the water body.

Next fill in the column using sand blocks to remove the water.

Dig out the sand blocks and empty the column.

Place four blocks of dynamite. If you can manage place them at the bottom, or alternatively you can also place them on the top layer, since they will fall down once ignited anyway.

Ignite the TNT blocks and run.

When the TNT explodes it will destroy the column of sand leaving an empty space, of two by two blocks, and as deep as the water body itself. This will cause water to flow in creating a small whirlpool.

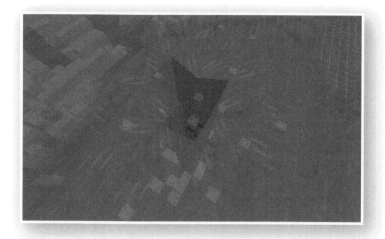

An alternative design is to create a column of sand of five by five blocks, and put a three by three block layer of TNT. The whirlpool created by this design is even bigger.

A few of these whirlpools created at the entrance to your base can act as effective choke points and mob traps.

Lava Floor trap

What you will need -

1. A dozen lava buckets
2. Carpet
3. Dispensers

A fun little trap that is a little hard to turn off once activated. This trap uses dispensers hidden amongst floor blocks, covered by carpet. In the dispensers are buckets of lava.

When the trap is triggered the dispensers spew the lava out, burning whoever is standing in the room.

The only way to clean the room is to place blocks on the lava sources on top of the dispensers. The carpet blocks need to be replaced each time the trap is activated because the lava burns them out. The lava buckets too need to be refilled (you will not lose the buckets, they can be reused).

First create a simple room, sized according to your own choice. Preferably a square room.

Replace a few floor blocks with dispensers. Place a trigger anywhere on the wall of the room.

Place lava buckets in each of the dispensers.

Connect the dispensers to the trigger.

Cover the floor using a carpet.

Now as soon as the unwitting player activates the trigger the lava spews out from the dispensers, filling the room, burning and in all likeliness killing whoever is in it.

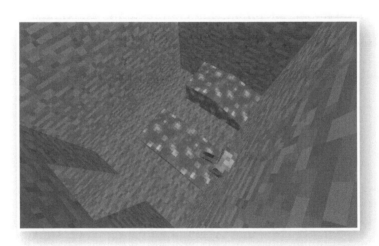

Lava Wall trap

What you will need -

1. Lava buckets
2. Paintings
3. Dispensers

This works on the same concept as the lava floor trap, dispensers spewing lava. The difference is that instead of the dispensers being on the floor, they are hidden in the walls, camouflaged using paintings.

When the trap is triggered lava flows out of the walls filling the room and killing anyone in it.

To create it simply place a painting on the wall. Once you get a painting the correct size (at least one by two blocks, a one block painting will not work) quickly break a block of wall behind the painting and then place a dispenser there.

Do not wait too long to place the dispenser because the painting will break and fall of within a few seconds.

Once this is done place the trigger, like a lever, and connect it to the dispenser.

As soon as the trigger is flipped, the trap is sprung and the lava spews out.

Crushing Traps

This section is devoted to traps which use blocks to suffocate the entities to death. All solid blocks can be used to suffocate players as well as mobs. To do so the blocks need to be forced into a space already occupied by the entity. This can either be done by dropping solid blocks like sand or gravel, or using pistons to push blocks.

It must be kept in mind that a player who is being suffocated can tap movement keys rapidly to escape, so while building such traps an enclosure of sorts should be built, that closes once the trap is activate, preventing the player from escaping.

Double Lever Gatehouse Trap

What you will need -

1. A doorway with enough space to build a small gatehouse around it.

2. Redstone dust

3. Two levers

4. Redstone Repeaters

5. A second doorway or piston controlled drawbridge

6. Iron doors for the doorway

In theory, this trap works on the same principle as the Double lever rail trap, but in this case the second lever is hidden in plain sight. The concept is simple. The entrance to the base has two stages. Say two doorways or a drawbridge.

Now each of the stages is controlled using a lever. Hidden above the doorway in the second stage are sticky pistons. If the lever for the second door is activated without closing the first door or the drawbridge, then instead of opening the door, the lever activates the piston, which push down the ceiling onto the players head, suffocating them.

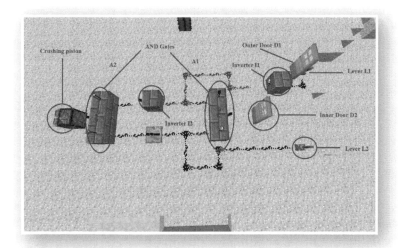

To make this work we will need to use two AND gates. Now this can be a little complex, so below is a basic diagram of how it's going to work. First try making this on open ground, just the simple circuit with a piston, two doors and the AND gates.

The outer door D1 is controlled by and connected to the lever L1. The inner door D2 is controlled by the AND gate A1. The piston is controlled by the AND gate A2. The inputs to the AND gates are provided using levers L1 and L2. The lever L2 is not directly connected to any of the doors.

The input to AND gate A1 is L2 and inverted L1. L1 is inverted using inverter I1 so that the door D2 only opens when the outer door D1 is closed.

The input to AND gate A2 is L2 and L1. Because we inverted L1's signal earlier, we need to invert it again using inverter I2. This means when D1 is open, and L2 is flipped to open D2, the piston will be activated.

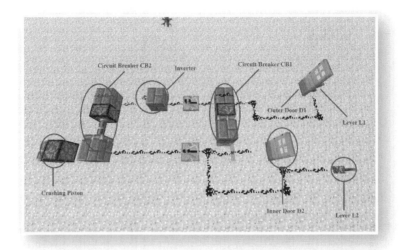

Another way to do this without using Gates, is by using two circuit breakers made out of sticky pistons. The plan is given below.

Again, we have two levers, L1 and L2. L1 is directly connected to outer door D1. L1's input is also used to control the flow of signal from Lever L2. L2's signal directly controls the inner door D2 as well as the crushing piston.

When L1 is activated and the outer door D1 is open, the circuit breaker CB1 gets activated, breaking lever L2's connection to inner door D2. At the same time because of the inverter changing L1's signal circuit breaker CB2 remains deactivated, permitting L2's signal to reach the crushing piston, thus activating it.

When L1 is deactivated and the outer door D2 is closed, the circuit breaker CB1 is deactivated, and flipping L2 opens the inner door D2. At the same the crushing piston is not activated because the circuit breaker CB2 breaks L2's contact with it.

Fun fact, the above circuit is a simple 1x2 DE-multiplexer, or decoder. The repeaters in the circuit are being used to regenerate the redstone signal and no more.

To actually use this to make a successful trap you need to make sure all the redstone circuitry is well hidden.

Below is a design using two iron doors. The circuits are out in the open in the images for ease of understanding, but make sure you cover them when you actually make this at your base.

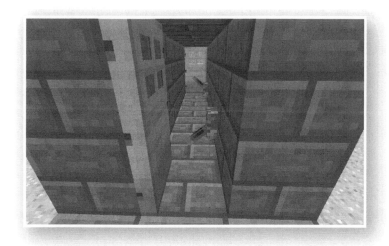

First build a small gate house, with a two block high tunnel between the inner and outer doors. The outer door is only operable from the inside. This tunnel is the only part that should be visible. Everything else must be later covered.

Connect the lever for the inner door to the door using redstone wiring as shown.

Place the sticky pistons one block above the ceiling and replace the ceiling blocks.

Connect the pistons to the lever for the inner door as shown.

Now when the lever is flipped, the inner door as well as the pistons get activated, so we need to add the circuit breakers connected to the lever for the outer door.

Add the first circuit breaker using a sticky piston as shown below.

This next part is a bit tricky, but mainly because we want to keep the assembly as compact as possible. Pay close attention to the picture. The second circuit breaker will be at ceiling level, connect to the outer door lever, via an inverter.

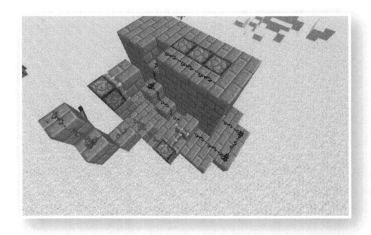

After this is done check the trap for consistency. Then cover up the circuitry. Make it into a gatehouse tower sort of structure if it looks too suspicious.

Your elaborate gatehouse crushing trap is ready.

Sand/Gravel Suffocation Trap

What you will need -

1. Sand or Gravel depending on what is more easily available
2. Sticky pistons
3. Redstone dust
4. Any trigger, preferably a lever

This is a simple trap where you place the activation trigger in plain sight. If you want you can disguise it as the trigger to open a door or dispense some items, or whatever strikes your fancy, but in truth it will just be a trigger to activate the trap.

The trap itself will involve a fake ceiling controlled using stick pistons. When triggered the ceiling will part, dropping a load of sand or gravel on the player below, suffocating them.

The downside of this trap is that every time it is triggered, you need to reset it manually, and replace the sand or gravel blocks.

To build it simply create a room two block wide and as many blocks long as you want. On the roof place sticky pistons in the manner shown below.

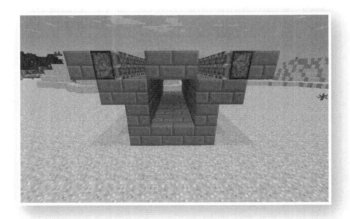

Place a lever to activate the trap.

Behind the lever on the other side of the wall (the side which will be hidden from all eyes), place a torch to create an inverter. This will help the ceiling stay in place when the lever is deactivated. As soon as it is activated the pistons will retract, pulling back the ceiling.

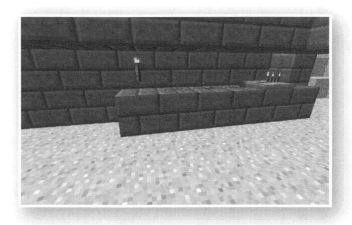

Connect the pistons to the circuit. Use repeaters to refresh the signal when required.

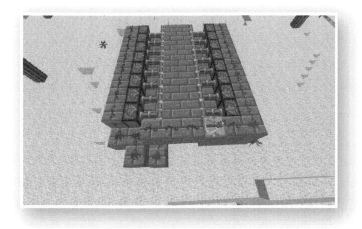

Place sand or gravel on top of the ceiling. Make a pile two blocks high.

Voila! Your trap is ready. Now whenever someone flip the lever, the ceiling will retract and the sand will descend upon the unfortunate victim.

Miscellaneous Traps

This section contains an assortment of traps which use killing methods like fall damage, or arrows. Many of these traps have no triggers and are more or less deep pits hidden artfully. These traps can be used inside the house, without occupying too much space or having to worry about other items being destroyed by killing methods like lava, water or TNT.

Fake Elevator trap

What you need -

1. Two to three sign boards
2. Two to three buckets of water
3. A deep hole

If you have not heard about what a water elevator is, then now is the time to learn. A water elevator is a stylish way to traverse great heights using water and sign boards. When the two are placed alternatively inside a long vertical shaft, they allow you to move up and down the shaft at considerable speed.

The same thing can be done using a ladder, but the water elevator consumes fewer hunger points when used, making it more efficient.

A simple water elevator is show below. Top block is water, below it is a sign board, then water again and another sign board below it and so on.

Where as a fake water elevator looks like what is shown below.

Basically you do not place the water blocks and sign blocks all the way down. You place just two or three layers and then leave the remaining shaft empty.

Due to obvious reasons this trap only works when used from above, so it is preferable if you have an underground base. In which case, you can use this as a fake entrance.

Make the water elevator and place a sign noting that it is the entrance to your base. Players will get into the water, expecting to float all the way down. But two tiers down they will realize that it is a trap. By then it will already be too late to climb back up and they will fall to their deaths.

If you place a hopper and chest assembly at the bottom, then you can even collect the dead players' loot later on.

Fake Sand Floor trap

What you will need -

1. A deep pit
2. Lots of sand
3. One sticky piston
4. Some redstone dust
5. A dozen torches
6. Carpet for hiding

This is an old design that uses the property of torches to be able to hold up sand and gravel blocks.

The trap is to be made in a separate room, which has a floor carpeted like the rest of the house so that the sand below is hidden. In the room is one trigger, a lever or a button, which can be placed so as to fool the player into thinking that it connects to a lamp or a door. In truth this trigger will activate a sticky piston, that pulls back a block on which the first torch is stuck.

When the block gets pulled, the torch breaks and falls, leading all the sand blocks it supports to also fall with a domino effect. This causes the floor to literally vanish from below they players' feet, causing them to fall to their death, provided the pit is deep enough.

The shaft below acts as the pit for us.

Place the first torch as shown below. On top place a sand block and three more torches.

Place more sand blocks with torches, tier by tier, as shown.

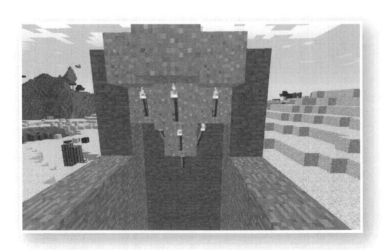

Repeat until you have a sand floor.

Cover the floor using carpet.

Place a trigger on one wall. Connect it to a sticky piston placed on the opposite of the block on which the bottom most torch is stuck.

As soon as the unsuspecting player activates the trigger, the block is pulled, breaking the torch, in turn breaking the whole floor.

Continuous Rapid Fire Arrow Trap

What you will need -

1. A few stacks of arrows
2. At least three dispensers
3. Four redstone repeaters
4. Redstone dust
5. A button or a pressure plate, or a trip wire
6. A sticky piston

This is probably the trap with the most straightforward kill method. Arrows. Just like those nasty arrow traps in RPGs like Skyrim.

The big different here is that while other arrow traps fire once and then stop, this trap fires arrows continuously until the dispenser is empty, so instead of using this where you expect only a few players to come, use it in a place like where there is a chance of an attack by at least half a dozen players together. If placed correctly, this trap can fire enough arrows, so fast that a dozen players in diamond armor would not last more than a minute.

The thing is that a dispenser fires an arrow every time it receives a signal. However most triggers send a signal only once. A button sends a signal and then stops. A lever sends a continuous signal, but sends it just once, so just one arrow is fired.

To get arrows to fire continuously and rapidly, we make use of a clock circuit, made using repeaters.

A simple clock circuit is given below. It is activated by a button and pulses rapidly after activation. The piston circuit breaker is used to stop further input signal from reaching the clock, to enable rapid pulsing. If continuous input is provided to the clock, for example from a lever, then the clock will not pulse.

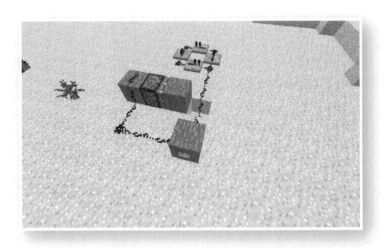

Now that you have a pulsing clock, all you need to do is connect a dispenser to it and place the arrows. Every time the clock signal reaches the dispenser one arrow will be fired. In practice this happens very quickly, making the arrows fire almost continuously.

Since this is a trap, when you actually place it try to hide the dispensers behind paintings. Also it might be better to use trip wire instead of a button so that unwary intruders might activate it without wanting to.

The only downside to this trap is that it uses up a lot of arrows, and is rather overkill, if used on one player. When used in an appropriate place however, the trap is extremely lethal.

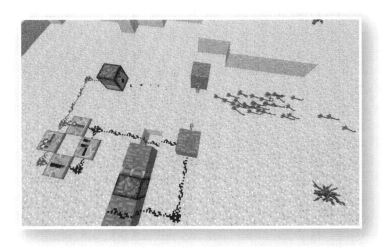

Tips and Tricks

1. All traps can be broken down into the three components, *Trigger, Mechanism* and *Method*.

2. Before you start building any trap, make sure you have enough space to place each of the three components. Plan ahead and clear ample space before you begin. This will save you from the frustration of redesigning the whole thing half way through.

3. Collect all the material you need before you begin making a trap.

4. When in doubt build a few practice models of the trap. Build the final model where you need it only once you are certain what to do.

5. Always be careful while working with lava traps, especially ones that utilize lava flow.

6. Redstone circuits can be tricky. Practicing them a few times before incorporating them into your traps is a good idea.

7. Always test your traps (with due safety measures of course), before you mark them ready.

8. At least once try to see and think from the point of view of the player you intend to use that trap on. This might give you insights into some of the weaknesses of the trap.

9. To make sure the trap is foolproof ask yourself some question. Are there any visible Redstone wires? Does the trigger look too obvious? Is the lure prominent enough? Is it too prominent and arouses suspicion? Once the trap is triggered is there time for the player to get away or disarm the trap? Does the whole trap structure fit in with the general surroundings or does it look unnatural?

10. Always keep innovating. Backup clocks circuits to take over if the main trap is disabled. Fail safe methods like TNT that blow up even if the trap is disabled. There is a wealth of additions that can be made to each and every trap design, to make it more complex and harder to disable and escape.

Final Words

As far as mob traps are concerned they usually involve the same basic design with variations to increase effectiveness. However a trap targeted towards players is different. A player trap in the end is a battle of wits. Yours against the player you intend to trap/ kill. No matter how complex your trap chances are that people will eventually find a loophole and a way to disable or avoid the trap. Thus it is important to keep trying new designs. Use your imagination and you can easily keep a step ahead of the competition.

Happy Gaming!

8866007R00041

Printed in Great Britain
by Amazon.co.uk, Ltd.,
Marston Gate.